2/19

Think Like a Scientist

COLLABORATE AND SHARE RESULTS

Joe Greek

Britannica Educational Publishing

IN ASSOCIATION WITH

ROSEN EDUCATIONAL SERVICES

Published in 2019 by Britannica Educational Publishing (a trademark of Encyclopædia Britannica, Inc.) in association with The Rosen Publishing Group, Inc.
29 East 21st Street, New York, NY 10010

Distributed exclusively by Rosen Publishing.
To see additional Britannica Educational Publishing titles, go to rosenpublishing.com.

First Edition

Britannica Educational Publishing
J.E. Luebering: Executive Director, Core Editorial
Mary Rose McCudden: Editor, Britannica Student Encyclopedia

Rosen Publishing
Amelie von Zumbusch: Editor
Nelson Sá: Art Director
Brian Garvey: Series Designer
Tahara Anderson: Book Layout
Cindy Reiman: Photography Manager
Karen Huang: Photo Researcher

Library of Congress Cataloging-in-Publication Data

Names: Greek, Joe, author.
Title: Collaborate and share results / Joe Greek.
Description: New York : Britannica Educational Publishing, in Association with Rosen Educational Services, 2019. | Series: Think like a scientist | Audience: Grades 3–6. | Includes bibliographical references and index.
Identifiers: LCCN 2017050387| ISBN 9781538302545 (library bound) | ISBN 9781538302552 (pbk.) | ISBN 9781538302569 (6 pack)
Subjects: LCSH: Science—Methodology—Juvenile literature. | Communication in science—Juvenile literature.
Classification: LCC Q175.2 .G74 2019 | DDC 507.2/1—dc23
LC record available at https://lccn.loc.gov/2017050387

Manufactured in the United States of America

Photo credits: Cover, p. 1 Zinkevych/iStock/Thinkstock; cover (top), back cover, interior pages background cetus/Shutterstock.com; pp. 5, 6 © Encyclopædia Britannica, Inc; p. 7 Nestor Rizhniak/Shutterstock.com; p. 9 Colin McConnell/Toronto Star/Getty Images; p. 10 William Thomas Cain/Getty Images; p. 11 Rawpixel.com/Shutterstock.com; p. 12 Kyodo News/Getty Images; p. 15 Joe Raedle/Getty Images; p. 16 Photos.com/Thinkstock; p. 17 A. Barrington Brown/Science Source; p. 18 Science History Images/Alamy Stock Photo; pp. 19, 20 NASA; p. 23 John P Kelly/The Image Bank/Getty Images; p. 24 Rubberball/Nicole Hill/Brand X Pictures/Getty Images; p. 25 corbac40/Shutterstock.com; p. 27 showcake/Shutterstock.com; p. 28 Jeffrey Coolidge/The Image Bank/Getty Images.

CONTENTS

CHAPTER 1

INTRODUCTION TO THE SCIENTIFIC METHOD AND WORKING TOGETHER

Scientists believe there is a natural explanation for most things. For any problem they see, they try to understand the cause so they can come up with a solution.

The process scientists use to solve problems is called the scientific method. Scientists start by finding out as much as possible about a problem. Then they make a hypothesis. A hypothesis is an attempt to explain the problem. They test the hypothesis with an **experiment**. Then they collect and analyze the results of the experiment, or the data. If the experiment does not support the hypothesis, the scientists think about the problem again and develop a new hypothesis.

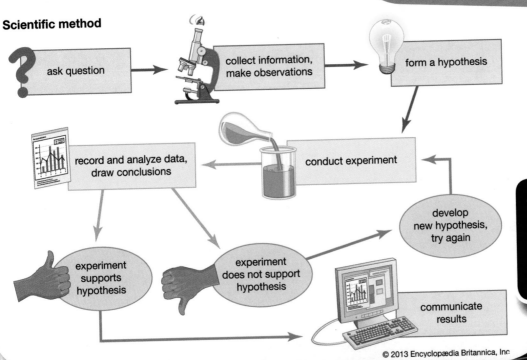

Scientific method

ask question → collect information, make observations → form a hypothesis → conduct experiment → record and analyze data, draw conclusions → experiment supports hypothesis / experiment does not support hypothesis → develop new hypothesis, try again → communicate results

This illustration shows the steps of the scientific method.

© 2013 Encyclopædia Britannica, Inc

Next, they test that hypothesis with a new experiment. If the experiment supports the hypothesis, other scientists repeat the experiment. If they get the same results, the hypothesis will be accepted as true until it can be proven false.

Scientists use information they learn from testing many hypotheses to develop scientific theories. A theory is a much broader explanation than a hypothesis. Scientists consider theories to be the best explanations for why some things happen. A theory may later need to be changed if scientists discover new information about the subject.

Nicolaus Copernicus developed an important theory about how the planets move around the sun.

Scientific research can involve a lot of work that is too difficult and time-consuming for one person. To speed up research and development of theories, scientists often collaborate and share the results of their work.

Collaboration makes it possible to approach the problem-solving process from many different points of view.

THINK ABOUT IT

Have you ever studied with a friend for a test? How is that similar to or different from scientists who collaborate together?

Collaboration and sharing information is a standard practice within the scientific community. In fact, many of the world's greatest discoveries would not have occurred if scientists chose to work alone rather than together.

CHAPTER 2

How Scientists Collaborate and Share Results

Scientists choose to work together and share research for many reasons. They often receive grants from governments and other organizations to fund their research. Grants may require multiple teams to collaborate and work toward the same goals. Additionally, research carried out by one team may require the help of another that has access to costly equipment that the first team does not.

Scientific research is often a slow process. It can take months and even years for a scientist to complete his or her work. For that reason,

Scientists often work together on research projects.

teamwork can help speed up the process by having individuals focused on certain tasks.

Many questions and challenges scientists think about are bigger than a single area of scientific knowledge. For that reason, another important benefit to collaborating and sharing results is that individuals and teams from different specialties can work together. Since most researchers are experts within a single area of science, collaboration is often necessary for complex projects.

So, how do scientists collaborate? They do so in two main ways. The chosen method will often depend on where the individuals or groups are located.

Scientists who live and work near each other may collaborate in person. In most cases, the researchers will have to get permission from their bosses. If they are allowed to work together, the scientists might share a research room, such as a

THINK ABOUT IT

Scientists work together because teamwork has many benefits. What other groups of people work together toward common goals?

Scientists at Temple University research ways to eliminate the deadly human immunodeficiency virus (HIV) from human cells.

laboratory at a university. They may also share the same equipment and tools.

When large distances separate scientists, it can be too costly and difficult to work in the same place. For example, it would take too much time for a scientist from Canada to travel back and forth to work with a scientist in France. In these types of collaborations, the researchers will work in separate laboratories. To work together,

Modern technology makes it easier for researchers to communicate and share data.

they will have to rely on technology and communication to be successful.

Much of the research that scientists work on is actually built on the results of others. It is important for scientists to share the results of their research. For one thing, it allows others to test and confirm or deny the results. Secondly, it can help scientists improve upon each other's work or make new discoveries.

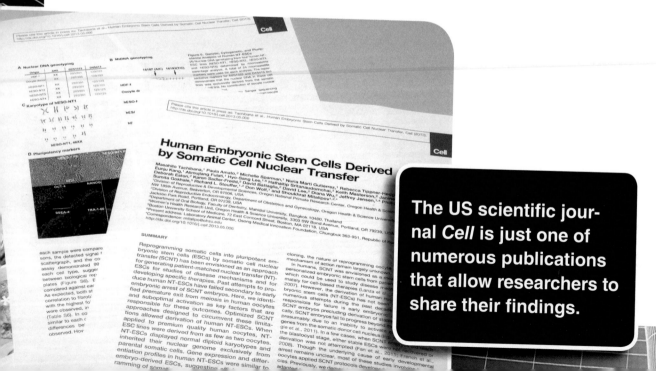

The US scientific journal *Cell* is just one of numerous publications that allow researchers to share their findings.

Scientists share their research in a number of ways. Scientific journals, for example, are magazines that contain articles about research and results. Scientists also share their research at conferences and speaking events. The internet is another place where scientists can share their results with peers through blogs, videos, and websites.

CHAPTER 3

SCIENTIFIC COLLABORATION IN ACTION

Often, scientists team up with others working in the same organization or laboratory. For example, many colleges have laboratories and programs dedicated to scientific research. Aside from professors, colleges also have researchers who work full-time. They will often bring on students to help with research projects. This helps the college meet its research goals while also giving its students real-world experience.

Additionally, scientists find collaborators by meeting others at professional events, such as conferences. Unfortunately, not all collaborations are successful. Different personalities and work styles can sometimes prevent researchers from working well together.

One of the most famous scientific collaborations occurred

COMPARE & CONTRAST

How might collaborating with students be different from collaborating with other professional scientists? How might it be similar?

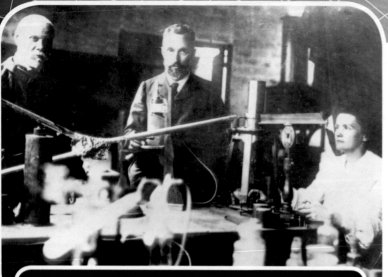

The research of Marie and Pierre Curie led to the discovery of two elements. Here they are in their lab with chemist Gustave Bémont (*left*).

between Marie and Pierre Curie. The Curies were a married couple who studied radioactivity in Paris in the late 1800s.

In 1896 another French scientist, named Henri Becquerel, discovered the unusual rays of energy given off by the element uranium. Marie Curie began studying the phenomenon, which she named radioactivity. In 1898 the Curies announced their discovery of radium and polonium. They named polonium after Marie's homeland of Poland. In 1903 the Curies shared the Nobel Prize for Physics with Becquerel.

After Pierre died in 1906, Marie carried on their research. In 1911 she won the Nobel Prize for Chemistry for isolating pure radium. She continued her study of radioactive substances and their use in medicine. Her Radium Institute in Paris became an important center of scientific research.

James Watson (*left*) and Francis Crick (*right*) discovered that the structure of DNA is that of a double helix. A model of a DNA molecule stands behind the two scientists in this 1953 photo.

In 1951, James Watson of the United States and Francis Crick of England decided to study the structure of DNA. The following year they started to build models to work out how the parts of a DNA molecule might fit

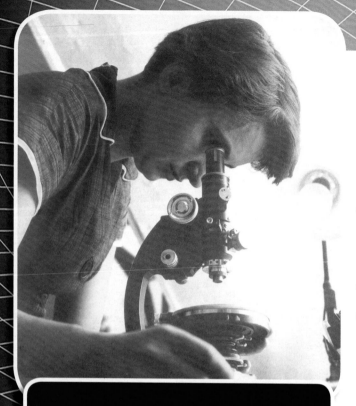

Rosalind Franklin's photograph of DNA helped Watson and Crick develop their theory about the structure of DNA.

together. None of their models were right.

In 1953 Watson and Crick saw an image of DNA taken by their colleague Rosalind Franklin using a special kind of process called X-ray diffraction. The image provided the missing information they needed to construct a model of DNA. It showed that the structure of DNA was a double helix (a shape like a twisted ladder).

The discovery proved to be one of the most important scientific break-throughs of the 1900s. It helped explain how evo-lution might work, and it has been used to develop greater understanding in all areas of genetics. Genetics is the study of how traits are passed from one generation to the next through genes, which are made up of DNA.

Today, scientists can collaborate beyond Earth. In fact, teams of international researchers are working together in outer space. The International Space Station (ISS) is operated by a group

Researchers from several different countries live and work together on the International Space Station.

of sixteen countries. Since its launch in 1998, ISS has been the home of numerous astronauts from around the world.

ISS crews gather data and carry out experiments. Many of these explore the effects of microgravity on humans, animals, plants, and other materials. Some of their experiments use microgravity to grow protein crystals. Research using these crystals might lead to more effective treatments

Researchers perform many different kinds of experiments aboard the ISS.

for cancer, diabetes, and other conditions. Other experiments conducted by ISS researchers might result in more accurate clocks, more useful weather predictions, and stronger metals.

THINK ABOUT IT

Scientists often make breakthroughs and discoveries by building on the work of others. Why is it important to share knowledge with others?

Researchers might share their results to gain acceptance by the scientific community. Scientists often speak at conferences and write articles for scientific journals that others can read. This is another kind of collaboration that helps spread scientific knowledge.

CHAPTER 4

YOU CAN COLLABORATE AND SHARE, TOO

Scientific collaboration and sharing results of research may sound like something only adults can do. However, students can collaborate with each other and share the knowledge they discover along the way.

Collaboration can be a fun way to learn with the help of others. There are many scientific things in the world students are curious about. By working together with peers, students can make discoveries together and share their knowledge with others.

Sharing research results in the classroom can happen in many different ways. Students may write a report that talks about an experiment and its results. They may even do a presentation in front of the class. Speaking in front of the class can also include performing an experiment in front of others.

There are many experiments that students can perform together without using a laboratory. With the help of an adult,

The classroom is a great environment to collaborate with other students and to learn more about science.

Sharing results with classmates helps to build a greater understanding of science.

COMPARE & CONTRAST

How is learning with others different from and similar to learning things by yourself? Do you have more fun working with others and helping each other out, or do you prefer to work alone?

you and your classmates can collaborate and discuss the results of the following experiments.

Experiment 1: Sink or Float

Objects sink or float because of a property called density. Density is how compact, or closely packed, an object is. If the object has a greater density than the water around it, the object will sink. Many objects float in salt water more easily than in fresh water because salt water is denser than fresh water.

To test this out, you and a partner will need two glass cups filled with warm water. In one glass, add ten tablespoons of salt and stir well.

EGG EXPERIMENT

Fresh Water - - - - →

← - - - - Salt Water

Adding salt to fresh water increases the density of the water. This allows objects such as eggs to float.

Next, place one raw egg in each glass. Take notes on what you and your partner see. Where do the eggs in each cup go? If you perform the experiment correctly, you will see that the egg in the fresh water sinks to the bottom. The egg in the salt water, however, will stay near the top of the water.

The density of the salt water is greater than the density of the egg, which causes the egg to float. An egg in normal water, however, is denser than the water and will sink.

Experiment 2: How Plants Drink Water

Most plants have roots that grow underground. The roots hold plants in place and help them absorb nutrients, such as water. Special tissues, called xylem, carry the water and other nutrients that are absorbed this way throughout the plant. How can we prove this?

In this experiment, you and your friends will each need one white carnation and a vase to put it in. With the help of an adult, each student will add twenty drops of different food colorings to each vase. Each vase will need to have only one food coloring used in it.

After the food coloring has been added, place a carnation in each vase and let it sit for one day. During the day, you can check the carnation to see if you notice any changes. You may see some changes occur, but after twenty-four hours you will see something very interesting.

The roots of a plant are located underground, where they can absorb water and nutrients from the soil.

You will notice that the carnations are no longer white. The petals of the flowers will change to the color of the drops that were added to the vases. This happens because xylem in the flower's stem carries the colored water in the vase up to the petals—the same way it carries water taken in through the roots to the rest of plant in nature. The dye just makes it much easier to see!

Once the experiment is complete, study the flowers with your friends. Did any particular color show up

Adding food coloring to the water in a flower vase can cause the petals to change color.

brighter than the others? Share your results with each other and your class.

As you grow up, you will find that collaboration and sharing results are not just limited to scientific research. When you have a job, working with others and sharing knowledge will help you succeed in different ways. The same will be true in different school subjects and even at home. The more you work with others and the more you share, you'll see that collaboration is a normal part of life.

THINK ABOUT IT

Teachers share knowledge with students to help them learn. Why is it important to learn and understand how the world around us works?

GLOSSARY

chemistry A science that deals with the composition, structure, and properties of substances and with the changes that they go through.

collaboration To work with others.

communication An act of exchanging information between two or more people.

community A group of people with common interests.

conference A meeting for discussion or exchange of opinions.

diffraction The bending or spreading of a beam of light, especially when passing through a narrow opening or by the edge of an object.

DNA The material that carries all the information about how a living thing will look and function.

grant An amount of money given by an organization, such as a government, for a specific purpose.

information Knowledge obtained from investigation, study, or instruction.

medicine A substance or preparation used in treating diseases and illnesses.

microgravity The condition of being weightless or of the near absence of gravity.

nutrient A substance that is essential to grow and maintain life.

peer A person of the same rank or class as another.

physics A science that deals with matter and energy and their actions upon each other.

radioactivity The giving off of rays of energy or particles by the breaking apart of atoms of certain elements.

research Careful study and investigation for the purpose of discovering and explaining new knowledge.

FOR MORE INFORMATION

Ardley, Neil. *101 Great Science Experiments.* New York, NY: DK Children, 2014.

O'Quinn, Amy. *Marie Curie for Kids: Her Life and Scientific Discoveries, with 21 Activities and Experiments* (For Kids). Chicago, IL: Chicago Review Press, 2016.

Parker, Steve, and Chris Woodford. *Science: A Visual Encyclopedia.* New York, NY: DK Children, 2014.

Science Year by Year: A Visual History, From Stone Tools to Space Travel. New York, NY: DK Children, 2017.

Wissinger, Mary. *Women in Chemistry: A Science Book For Kids!* St. Louis, MO: Genius Games, 2017.

WEBSITES

K12Science
http://www.k12science.org/materials/k12/technology/online-collaboration
Twitter: @FollowStevens, Facebook: @Stevens1870

SciDevNet
http://www.scidev.net/global/policy-brief/international-scientific-collaboration
-a-quick-gui.html
Twitter, Facebook: @SciDevNet

ScienceDirect
http://www.sciencedirect.com
Twitter: @ScienceDirect, Facebook: @Elsevier.ScienceDirect

INDEX